THE TRUTH ABOUT ISLAM

Mohammed Kilani

authorHOUSE®

AuthorHouse™
1663 Liberty Drive
Bloomington, IN 47403
www.authorhouse.com
Phone: 1-800-839-8640

This book is a work of non-fiction. Unless otherwise noted, the author and the publisher make no explicit guarantees as to the accuracy of the information contained in this book and in some cases, names of people and places have been altered to protect their privacy.

First published by AuthorHouse 11/12/2009

ISBN: 978-1-4490-5027-6 (e)
ISBN: 978-1-4490-5026-9 (sc)

Printed in the United States of America
Bloomington, Indiana

This book is printed on acid-free paper.

"What is the hardest thing of all?
That which seems the easiest.
For your eyes to see,
That which lies before your eyes."

Goethe

Table of Contents

To every soul, every being and every atom in this existence, you are my teacher.

Introduction

These words have resided in my heart for years.

Seeing and recognizing the very little of knowledge I had made me hesitate however. Though the resonance of the truth was seamlessly clear, I was aware of some inner struggles I was yet to challenge and encounter, the struggles which came to build up throughout the years of my life. And so I feared that they would creep their way into my words, and into the understanding I am to communicate. I wasn't at peace enough, and so waited for some sort of an evolution in my awareness before I could be able to let this potential flow.

Though waiting to get to a single truth, a state of 'enlightenment', I failed to see that even4 this desire was another mind trick arising from the same struggles I was contemplating to resolve.

Our life now is the outcome of years of an unnatural way of living, a state of strange madness, a state of blindness to our very basic instincts. Everyone seems to be engaged in an endless material race, never stopping to see that the point is being entirely missed, that if one isn't at peace at the very moment, if one's present is miserable, then whatever being pursued becomes of no value.

People are following countless theological and religious teachings – almost blindly – untiring to stop for a moment and contemplate the value or meaning of the practices being performed. Others have just stopped caring and surrendered to this material realm, declaring spirituality to be mere fiction. Everyone seems to be engaged in his own practice, a practice he argues to be the true path, hence the ever increasing divisions between the people of the world, even between those who claim to belong to the very same sect.

Truth is simple however, and if we allow ourselves to snap out of our turbulent thoughts into a mere moment of silence, we would be able to see the higher truth that we are missing. This book is intended to shed some light on the reasons which have kept us stuck into the same endless cycle for thousands of years. Perhaps the integral perspective here will help enlighten us to what would evolve us out of the mindset with which we seem to have come stuck, it is left for you to see and practice, truth is everywhere, it is us who are failing to see.

This is not a book for Muslims; Islam is not a closed religion. This book is for everyone. The title, stories and examples are only meant to help deliver the book more to those whom are in most need for it. The same truth is found everywhere, in almost every religion, practice and cult. We are now the product of a universal mindset that has prevailed for a very long time. It's time to see.

I am yet aware of the little of knowledge I have, but I know that these words can at least enlighten a heart, and for that reason they have flown.

Emotions

Once, I spent time observing the motherhood of a cat to its children. At their early years, she guarded them like no human mother would do, and yet at later stages forced them to leave her in order to grow responsible on their own.

The seemingly simple incident hit me with great significance as I could see a live demonstration for the difference between pure divine love and confused human emotions.

Humans are capable of a higher and free form of intellectual thinking, unlike animals, whose intelligence is limited to their instincts. This isn't necessarily a good thing to us, it is so as long as we recognize and animate with our natural instincts, and so remain in harmony with nature and with the universe. We however seem to be sinking away from that harmony, allowing imposed thoughts and turbulent emotions to take the drive. When we animate against our natural instincts, we become a destructive force to ourselves and to that which is around us, simply because we step out of the natural cycle, sinking even below our fellow creatures whom we might be belittling.

This higher form of intelligence we have, is supposed to be a tool with which we help elevate our consciousness to a finer level. We are supposed to be a creature that brings more harmony, who affirms the natural flow, not drive things to a worse condition as we are doing now.

Humans should – as other creatures are – be living in a great state of grace and joy, instead, we are now the most neurotic and miserable creature on the planet, and strangely, our so-called intelligence isn't helping us recognize why.

Animals do not have emotions as we do, their feelings are a natural flow of their instincts, they can't be neurotic about something for a simple reason that they express whatever they feel immediately, not allowing any repressions to accumulate leading a mental illness. Human children, at their early stages, are just like that. They cry or laugh whenever they feel like it. Their behavior is natural, and with that natural flow of expression they hold no grudges, and their energy is constantly creative and at peak.

A human mother, claiming love for her children, becomes neurotic about everything. She becomes overprotective, binding, fearful, and would prevent her children from flowing their natural creative expression. Most mothers maintain such behaviors for the whole course of their lives, even after their kids get married and become old. Divine love isn't the driving force here, what's taking action is a reservoir of deep rooted emotional wounds and pains, rooting even to the earliest years of the mother's life, and hence causing such neurotic attachments and fears to arise. Otherwise, the mother will just do what she has to do, and then would continue the course of her life. She won't fear taking lead of her life, and won't need an attachment to fill her void. She will be simply natural.

Fathers do the same, inflicting their conflicts unto their children through the practices of power, control, direction, guilt etc.

And so the cycle continues, conflicts are passed, and we keep swerving farther and farther from our natural instinctual behavior.

It's extremely important to see the difference between neurotic emotions and natural feelings. Natural feelings are responses to the present moment, never exceeding to an over-reaction caused by a tied emotion that hasn't been expressed in the past. We need to be extremely aware, as almost all human actions nowadays are a product of such tied emotions. This is exactly why we have diverged and sunk into where we are now, becoming destructive to ourselves and to the world around us. This can't be emphasized enough, this is not an over simplification, it is the 'root' cause. We need to release our hindering emotions in order to become an expression of the present, and in order to step back to our natural harmonious state.

We are, until are at balance with our emotions, incapable of true love. Great scientists like Wilhelm Reich stated that 'natural love' has been extinguished from the hearts of human beings since more than 10000 years, that's when humans started repressing their emotions in the name of living up to a social standard, belief system or a religious sect.

Therefore in order to start living, in order to be able to see the truth, one must first be freed of all his emotional conflicts. When that is done, every step becomes a divine step, a reaction to the present, an act of nature and a path through which one lives the role he's supposed to play in this existence.

Beyond our surface, beyond the personality we communicate through, lays a deep pool of wounds and conflicts. These emotions - when existing - become the driving force of human's actions and the inhibitors of his awareness. With the repression of such wounds, we allow emotions like pride, jealousy, hatred and anger to arise, making it almost impossible to submit to a truth when is seen and felt. The more restrictive and non-accepting a society is, the more its nation sinks further in ignorance.

We fail to see that almost all our actions – even the seemingly noble ones – are just symptoms and reactions to such wounds. A moral person might follow what he believes to be a noble cause, being it a religious sect, a cause or an act of self sacrifice for the benefit of others, not seeing that his actions are just desperate attempts to feel accepted by others. To those who care less about social acceptance, moral and immoral behaviors might sound alike, allowing their emotional hunger to act in whatever way - even the worst of which.

Though a moral person is yet closer to the natural instinct, both cases would eventually lead to the same thing. As long as the actions are a product of one's emotions, they would only reflect their source; the individual will keep slumping, and his actions – coming from an imbalanced place – will only be destructive. Until one stops to contemplate the source of his actions, until one sees the real driving force, no natural order will take place and people will keep running in the same endless circle.

True actions come from a state of thoughtlessness, a state of being in the present, of knowing one's purpose, and of letting go and allowing the natural flow to take place. In this place, in the present, no past incidents or future longings have control on one's thoughts and actions.

Almost all religious disciples fail to see that they live a state where they believe themselves to be better than others, having a message to deliver to the world.

By that very thought, by failing to see that their need to guide is only another way to feel more worthy, they fall into the same trap. The product, evidently, leads not to a single truth, a single world, but to divided sects each trying to prove themselves right.

To the willing observer, truth can't be simpler. Children care neither about their race nor about the religion their parents came to adapt, at least until they are initiated into a sect or a belief system.

And so, the first step for us to be able to see the truth of things is to let our emotional expression flow out, to be a true expression of whatever is inside us, to be simply honest with ourselves and with others. When that is done, our natural state is restored, we are back like children are, our instinct takes over the incessant thoughts and no pride, anger and emotion would stand in the way of our development into the graceful state we should all be experiencing.

Can only be This Way

Who is God?

In our early years, the majority of us learned about God from a parent, a school teacher or a mentor. Naturally as all children do, we wondered what this great entity is, where it resides, how it looks like and how it can be better understood.

These wonders however are usually shut out by the statements that we shouldn't ask such questions, or won't be able to comprehend God with our current mental abilities.

And so years pass by, either indulging us in a great deal of practice that we mostly don't understand, or causing an internal conflict which usually wards us off the very concept hence building communities that refuse the very idea of religion.

It's only natural for these conflicts to happen. An act that is not understood can't be done wholeheartedly, and by trying to forcibly convince one's self that the way being followed is the right one, it becomes only a matter of time before an emotional shock would shake this imposed belief off its unfounded base.

Throughout history, we've all witnessed each and every common belief system turning into countless sects, each claiming to have the ultimate truth, pitying or fighting others for their ignorance.

If one would comment, the only thing to state would be that "all these parties are missing the point". If God is the creator of this existence, if God is the one and only, and the origin of all things, then every single atom in the universe must be a spring of this single point, of God, and hence must be God. Wouldn't God's way be a way that unites people beyond boundaries and sects, without judgments of any form?

All the current movements, been religious, social or even spiritual sound like an act of emotion rather than an act of God. An emotion, be it anger, fear, need for power, feelings of worthlessness or even love (the conditional form) are acts of ignorance. They can't lead to a harmonious world.

If we go with the instinct, we will see that the only possible way is the way that would bring us in harmony with this existence, the way that recognizes the unity of all people and creatures just as they are. We are all part of the very same divine spark.

A collective state of peace can only be attained if people are at peace with themselves, which only starts with fixing one's own conflicts. This requires one to be truly honest with himself as our conflicts have grown so deep with our control-obsessed practices. This takes true courage, a courage far greater than that which we base on mere physical acts. A person can be the greatest war hero, only to discover at last that he was only living up for his father's expectations, or trying to fill up a deep feeling of personal void.

Getting to know ourselves, getting to see the source of our feelings is the first step one can take in any spiritual or religious journey. This is the journey which would melt our emotionally based actions into the divine form of action. The form which sprouts out of letting go, knowing and doing one's role in this existence, be it whatever it be.

Other creatures, organisms and objects around us, are living constantly in that state; they all know and live their roles. Humans, by stepping back to that level, can then start using their higher intelligence in a way that would enlighten the world further, raise its vibrations to a higher state, rather than be destructive to it as we do now.

It's sad to admit that, right now, humans are probably the lowest in consciousness between all their fellow creatures. A small ant can enlighten the observer in mere minutes of observation, for it lives its moment, its role and is living the oneness with existence. Humans on the other hand, are gone astray with their incessant thoughts, words and actions not knowing that they are given out by their past wounds and future plans. So rarely we find a true master who is living in the moment, the present, beyond the past and future, and is only flowing whatever he is needed to do, flowing out the Godly presence.

In our youth, we have been taught a nice piece of prayer:

God be in my head, and in my understanding;

God be in mine eyes, and in my looking;

God be in my mouth, and in my speaking;

God be in my heart, and in my thinking;

God beat mine end, and at my departing.

We so rarely contemplate however, that this is a literal example encouraging us to understand how God becomes us whenever we let go wholeheartedly. God has always been in us, he is the single point from where all existed. It's just our thoughts that are standing in the way of this divinity to animate through us. This is not a metaphor.

Whoever first taught this prayer knew that if we become children of the moment, our actions become a living flow of God, he becomes our hands because the hand will no more serve a thought, but will play a natural role, and so the same for every other part of our being.

By taking this first step, by letting go and living the moment without any ties to the past or future, we step to the level of all other creatures which are always living their divine role.

In our bodies, if cells start behaving in a strange way, disobeying their natural role and thus destructing the body, we call that a cancerous formation. Humans, being driven now by emotions and not by their natural instinct, are becoming exactly the same to this planet. Earth is a living organism and humans are part of this organism's constitution, and unless we are back to flow naturally, Earth will start doing the cleanse itself.

Only when we free our motives and actions from their emotional origin, we can start using this mind we have in a way that would refine the universe and raise it to the next level.

If that happens, life will no more be the way we see it now, in the first stages the world will appear to be a land of living saints, it will bloom, people will live in utter peace, and gradually our material existence will be raised beyond duality into a higher form of existence. Though hard to imagine in the beginning, it's very much like stepping from a lower frequency into a higher one, and that step is only taken when the collective consciousness of people changes, when everyone lives his inner evolution, when no judgment prevails, when we see God in everything.

For example, instead of having happiness and sadness – the dual cases – we will be at peace, right the middle.

Our limited knowledge has blinded us to the fact that God can either be everywhere or nowhere. Therefore, no matter how solid and convincing this material reality might appear to us, we miss the fact that this is all part of that single point from where all sprouted. God is everywhere.

Humans however, have declared themselves to be above all other creatures, and with that gave themselves permission in the ugliest form to utilize 'needlessly' whatever they can take, in order to fulfill the unending hungers they have, these hungers however can never be fed until one sees beyond the superficial urge into the real motive causing them to exist.

Arguments and mind tricks will keep arising in trying to justify and provide convincing answers. We will keep trying to convince ourselves – and act to prove – that we are better than others. I'm better than him because I'm a Muslim and he's a Christian. I'm better because I'm white and he's black, educated and illiterate, and so on. Only the instinct however, only the natural thought that is not bound to an emotion, is capable of providing an ultimate answer, that which can unconditionally assert our origin and our common nature.

An emperor who lives a life of luxury beyond imagination might suffer the worst kind of depression, and the poorest of the poor might lead a life of peace and satisfaction. The moral is clear, material possessions have nothing to do with our fulfillment.

In most cases, the people who seem to have an endless need for material or social expansion to be happy are just in need to put themselves above other individuals to feel worthy. By looking deep into their feelings, they can start observing where this need for validation comes from, and what these material and social obsessions are filling.

Other cases come disguised in a more ambiguous form, one can observe cases where people tend to withdraw themselves from the material life (as in many spiritual practitioners), then preach people that dropping the material, that humbleness, is the way to the spirit. In their very preach, it's clearly seen that their arguments come from the same place, the need for them to prove themselves right, and hence – unconsciously – giving themselves a value to fill where a void is present. Soon as well, a falsely founded base would cause more damage than good, and it's only a matter of time before the whole method collapses. This, I believe, is exactly why almost all religions and methods are soon to divide into various sects and ways.

Needless to say, a quick look around can show the great conflicts between the believers in the very same thing. There must be something wrong with the foundation, otherwise sects will easily be united, religions will become one, and people will be as they were always intended to be, brothers and sisters, and children of this existence.

A very rich man once went to a great master, saying that he wants to change the world, and wants to use his money to bring peace to it. The great master looked at him silently, in a loving but almost a pitying look. The rich man noticed and exclaimed "I'm very rich, I can do many things with this wealth I have, why are you looking at me as if I was a poor man?", the master responded "Unless you are aware, unless you know yourself, then every act of yours will bring more ignorance rather than light to the world."

Little money, flowing from an enlightened heart, is worth more than millions coming from a wounded one. The first will grow and flow to serve the existence while the other will serve only what it's serving, an emotion.

Therefore, by throwing all the boundaries we have accumulated over the years, we will see that God is indeed everywhere, that all people are perfect exactly the way they are, their presence teaches a lesson even if they didn't learn their own.

Only being aware of our thoughts and acts is needed, this way no mistakes will be repeated, lessons will be learned and we will grow in the right direction.

Worlds beyond Worlds

We have grown to accept this material world as the only tangible form of existence, out of its seeming solidity we are misguided by our senses not to think farther.

Though religious practitioners usually believe in the existence of other worlds, of heaven and hell and of eternity, most of them have declared these planes to be part of the divine knowledge, and stated that they can only be accessed after death, hence again limiting their perception to this material plane.

It needs not great thinking to see that our senses only access a small part of this existence. Physics has shown that our sight can only see a fraction of what can be seen, that our ears can only hear a very small range of frequencies, and so on for our other senses. Our access to this material world, when using our physical senses, is extremely limited.

Although it's convenient to believe that existence is limited to what we can sense, in reality it isn't. In this age, we are all aware of technology utilizing various forms of the unseen to transmit messages all over the world.

Radio, television, satellite transmission are few examples of technologies that came to exist by utilizing such knowledge.

Through a special instrument, like the radio, we are able to receive and experience such vibratory ranges. Some animals can naturally hear and see into an expanded range that is above or below what we can naturally experience.

This is just a small example of what exists beyond our direct physical contact, of forms that we have come to confirm using special instruments. It doesn't mean however that we have come to know all that exists.

By unlocking our sight to perceive farther, we enable ourselves to examine the effects of the unseen. This is exactly what has been done by the great scientists of history who refused to accept the known notions and followed their own instincts with which they were able to make history's greatest discoveries. Instead of accepting the incomplete answers their society provided, they went for better answers and for deeper examination of the observed phenomenon.

This is exactly what we are doing here, instead of surrendering to the answers we have been taught, thus standing at a point where it's impossible to form an integral knowledge of this existence's dynamics, we are invited to learn more and answer our questions by examining the effects of what we don't normally sense, until we are able to form a better understanding, and until experience replaces 'believing' with 'knowing'.

As we grow to understand more, there comes a point where our questions are answered and an integral picture of this existence is finally formed, the ancients called that state 'enlightenment', a state of being one with the divine knowledge, and of claiming back what's naturally ours. The shift is a shift of awareness, existence is always the same.

Almost all the great masters have done the very same thing. Stories have been told of Mohammed spending complete months alone in the cave of Hira, of Jesus traveling the east, of Buddha leaving his fortune to embark a journey of self discovery and of countless similar accounts where people leaped from their cultural and religious teachings to answer the questions their society failed to give convincing answers to.

The vastness of this material world is alone striking, we are only aware of a small part of what's around us, of this material world we live in. Our access is limited to this Earth, where Earth is a dot in a galaxy, and a galaxy is a dot in a sea of other galaxies.

This vastness however, all this existent matter, creatures, light and sound, are only forms of energy vibrating at a specific rate, we know that matter is only seemingly solid, atoms are almost all empty, there are no small solid objects that form our tables, chairs and bodies, it's all just forms of vibrating energy.

Therefore, we are invited here to think that if all this material existence vibrates at a specific rate, then other realities might exit, and by changing the rate at which we vibrate we might even be able to access and experience these realities.

The physicists of today are starting to confirm these theories, quantum physics declares the existence of parallel realities, and leading physicists like Stephen Hawking are writing actual equations that theorize the interaction with these realities.

Spiritual practitioners on the other hand, have confirmed the existence of these other realities, of these other worlds and finer forms of existence since the earliest of time. They needed no scientists to confirm what they experienced because they have developed the awareness and the ability to willfully raise their vibratory state thus shifting their existence into another form of reality.

Carl Jung, a well known psychoanalyst, shocked his inner circle when he suddenly accepted the existence of these other forms of reality after he experienced a temporary clinical death. He publically declared that "*death is not the end*", that "*in our altered states we are able to access the past and future, to go beyond space and time*".

Jung, in his clinical death, experienced departing from earth, and saw planet earth from outer space, he stated that he was fully aware, that it was as clear to him as this reality is to us. The experience didn't last long as his body was being vitalized and soon enough he woke up back in the clinic after his heart started beating again.

Later on, whenever Jung was asked whether he believed in these forms of existence, said: "*I know, I don't believe.*"

Jung is one scientist that people respect in today's mainstream. Countless similar accounts have taken place, all declaring the very same thing.

It's almost confirmed by scientists today that this material reality we experience is just matter vibrating at a specific rate, going up or down in the frequency of this vibration we shift our existence into other parallel worlds and realities.

In sleep, because our thoughts are stiller than they are when awake, we experience other realities which we call dreams. Sometimes dreams are just unconscious experiences of repressed emotions that manifest in that altered reality. But at other times, people might see in their dreams what we can only account as paranormal, for it contradicts with our common knowledge. People might see into the future, might be given insights, a higher piece of knowledge that is later confirmed to be true, though unknowing how it came to be channeled.

Sleep is a form of meditation, only it's an unconscious experience most of the time. When we start falling into sleep, our conscious state starts getting stiller and stiller, until at one point, our existence – or consciousness – snaps out of this body and into another reality.

We rarely remember our dreams, because we're not usually interested in maintaining a conscious state when we fall into sleep. Our experiences are hence usually limited to manifestations of emotions, of thoughts that have been repressed.

Spiritual practitioners alternatively, have learned how to enter this stiller vibratory state consciously, and so they are able – after snapping out of the physical body – to consciously control their movement in these parallel worlds.

Soon enough, the traveler starts learning more and more about his conscious states. Being unbound by the physical body, it becomes apparent that the thought is the only mean of control there. In the material world, thoughts are still the means by which we control our reality; the effect is just cruder to experiment with. Try however to raise your hand in the air, move it right and left perhaps, and while doing so just try to contemplate the real force that is moving the hand, sure it isn't the mind as we don't seem to be processing any intellectual thoughts while we move our hand. The motion seems to happen naturally as we pass the intention to move, as we 'become' the state. It's important to try and contemplate.

Thoughts are the creators of our reality, even in this crude material presence. It takes more time compared to our finer states, but still functions in the exact same way.

The experimenter will clearly observe how our present thoughts are the only thing in control. Reality is a reflection of that state, past and future simply creep into our present thoughts causing our reality to be a reflection of our fears and doubts.

This material existence, in its crude state where dualities are experienced, have come to exist only because – collectively – the thoughts of people have fallen into a very low state. Instead of letting go and living the present, people are now living in fear, past wounds and future longings, hence driving our reality to become the very fears we are trying to avoid.

Unless we get to know ourselves, that which starts with releasing our unconscious feelings, we won't be doing any good to ourselves and to this world. Until we do that, our thoughts will still be controlled by our emotions, and our world will naturally be a reflection of that.

In this world, we live a dual reality, where we experience happiness and suffering, pain and pleasure, positive and negative, male and female, time, and space. By keeping ourselves locked in this state, we prevent ourselves from seeing that these states, hard as it be to imagine, are just existing forms of creation. Scientists are now seeing that even time and space are forms of existing matter. Spiritual teachers have confirmed this throughout the ages, perhaps it's time for the mass to experience this too, perhaps it's time now for a collective shift in the way we think, and hence the world we experience.

In religious teachings, we hear of heaven, a place where there is no time, where one is granted whatever he wishes, where one lives an eternal state of peace. We also learn that this place is accessed after death if one is pure and virtuous.

Indeed, in death, when one departs from his body, his conscious presence becomes free to wander in a finer vibratory state, in which our conscious thoughts are the instant creator of our reality. Thus, if one had peaceful and loving thoughts, he would exist in a reflection of these thoughts, or what we call heaven. If he had the opposite, he would live in a crude place where suffering and hatred are present, a reflection of his inner thoughts as well, that which we call hell.

Therefore, it has nothing to do with how long one prays at night, or how much money one gives away. Our thoughts are our thoughts, and they are the driver of our reality, be it now or after death. Mohammed always stated that virtue weighs more than all the religious acts combined. He did communicate true divine knowledge, and so did all the other great masters. It is us who failed to contemplate the essence and have fallen into the traps of our internal struggles. It's time to see where our actions really originate, be them religious or personal.

The interested individual might wonder how these finer states of reality are accessed, though – knowingly – there are no current scientific means to do so, it's fairly simple to access such states consciously.

Material reality is just existence at a specific vibratory range. When we are awake for example, our conscious presence vibrates at this reality's rate, hence allowing our conscious presence to exist in this physical body.

When we meditate, as in when we fall asleep, our thoughts get stiller and stiller, and our vibratory state – being controlled by our thoughts – slows down. At a certain level, a snap happens and one's presence is freed from the physical body as his consciousness is stilled enough to vibrate in the range of a finer state.

In meditation, this practice is usually accomplished willfully by sitting in a comfortable position, relaxing the body bit by bit until it's completely relaxed, and then by simply remaining in and maintaining a thoughtless state. Being thoughtless, we slow down our vibrational state, and at a point, one snaps out of his physical body into a higher state of reality, where one can practice further control on his thoughts, observing how they interact with the reality we experience.

Meditation is easiest to be practiced in the early times of the morning, right before dawn. Many people in fact experience quick snaps out of their physical bodies at the early moments of waking up. One simply feels that he has no control over his body, as if it has completely frozen. Usually a strong high frequency sound is also heard, and to whom isn't aware of what's happening, it can be quite frightening. One might start praying, thinking that something is taking over his body, until eventually, the senses are restored.

In reality, this is just a state where our conscious state – out of stillness – is forced out of the physical body. At that point, if one wishes, he can start using his thoughts to navigate the finer realities. It takes a lot of practice to be in total control of such navigation, but each experience is enough to teach a lesson.

Returning to the physical body is a matter of wanting so, thoughts are the driving force, and as long as the physical body is in a healthy state to accept the consciousness back, one can willfully return.

By embarking this journey, one will be able to further learn and understand how this universe animates, how and why this physical world came to exist. It's wise however to maintain a very high state of awareness especially when embarking such journeys, as these worlds can be full of temptations that might play on our weaknesses, hence slowing down our conscious development.

The universe is so vast. The billions of galaxies we experience are just part of the material world, a world among other worlds each vibrating at a different rate. We are simply invited to see what we are missing by locking ourselves into perceiving just what is directly seen.

In the beginning one would learn that he is unbound by this physical body, that there are worlds finer than this we experience, that our thoughts are the creators of our reality. And later on, one would start experiencing even finer states, where time and space seem to have collapsed into a single present moment, an eternity, where mind ceases to exist and finally when one is united back with the source of all this existence.

Scientists in our age have found ways to force such experiences by stimulating the pineal gland in the brain with specific chemical combinations. Many scientific studies are taking place, Rick Strassman, author of the book "DMT: Spirit Molecule" has carried out many experiments proving that the experiences of his subjects, who took the stimulating drug, are taking place in altered realities, confirming beyond doubt that they weren't just dreamlike hallucinations.

Ancients have also used sacred drinks to help them experience these states and communicate with higher beings. These traditions still survive in some tribal cultures. In the Amazon's rain forests, many people are reporting the very same experiences after they paid a visit to some tribal teachers and took permission to try the sacred drink.

It's urged however, that the meditative state should take place naturally, not with the help of a drug or a drink. They should take place when one is consciously ready. No shortcuts can be taken in the spiritual development, our thoughts – again – are our thoughts, and our present emotions will stand in the way of our development, even slump us downwards if they were not realized.

All that exists is in the present, this place and this moment, and thus, we should also be aware – as it can be a trap as well - that experiencing the universe should not be a need, but a natural state that we live as we grow into a more aware state. One should not look for an experience, the only thing we should be doing is living in the conscious present, this way we are able to be the divine self that we are.

Surrendering to the present isn't an easy task, for it to occur; one is faced by his personal challenges, and is required to resolve whatever he accumulated during the course of his life. It's indeed a great invitation for self-discovery.

Why did God Start Religions?

For a person who follows a specific religion, the answer might seem easy, "because it's the true way", "the natural path", etc.

But one is challenged to look further, to try and find a truly satisfying answer especially that all religions seem to have something common in essence.

In my youth, I remember being taught by a teacher in school that Islam is the only true religion and that Muslims are the only ones who would be able to access heaven after death, even the ones who misbehaved, though would be punished first for their misdeeds.

At the time, I couldn't but wonder, the first question that came was: "What if there was a bad Muslim, and a good Christian, will the Muslim still be the one to reside in heaven?", the teacher answered: "One can't enter heaven unless he declares Islam.". Startling as it was, I went for the next logical question: "Suppose someone lived in the forest, was never introduced into any religion, yet was extremely virtuous and helped all whom were around him. Still he would not access heaven?", the teacher responded with the same answer.

This isn't necessarily what all religious teachers are saying, the majority of the fundamental teachers – not only in Islam – declare almost the same thing.

As a child, I couldn't imagine how this would be fair, though I understood many of the truths that are presented in the Islamic religion, this however was one of many things that revealed to me that our knowledge is suffering a sort of limitation, an ignorance to something clearly logical.

I also wondered why God would start a religion, then present another one, and then another one, and another, each with teachings that differ – in the direct sense – from the former.

I saw how consumed people were in empty religious acts, some would pray all night, some would fast all year long, some would claim humbleness and simplicity, while in all cases, it was clear that a lot of them showed no or very little grace in their everyday life.

It was clear that this can't be what religion is all about. The way I could perceive it, included religion being a path that would bring people out of their ignorance and into a true state of knowledge, a collective unity, enlightenment, and utter peace. That, simply, wasn't what I was seeing.

I was fortunate enough not to rebel and refuse the whole idea, I did see the truths behind the words, the evidences and the insights all which made it clear that beyond the ignorance in the application, a truth is desperate to be communicated.

Soon enough, I started observing the striking similarities between Islam and the other major religions, them being Christianity and Judaism. It was apparent that, in essence, they were all saying the exact same thing.

Later on, I also started observing that these resemblances are also present in many other religions and methods, the wisdom of the ancient philosophers, the words of past and modern scientists and the teachings of eastern mystics all in essence communicated the same thing, they all must have hit upon the same truth, and so it was striking to me how we have grown to declare all these parties ignorant.

There was no need for someone to tell me that I was going in the right or the wrong direction. This logical chain was the only possible way for things to make sense to me. And so I proceeded, despite the great taboos and closed mindedness where I lived, that declared Islam, and particularly the Sunni sect to be the only path for salvation.

It was apparent to me that a higher knowledge is to be pursued here, a higher knowledge that united all those who embarked journeys of self discovery and mystical knowledge. It was obvious that we weren't the only ones to know, the ignorance started to get more and more vivid.

At that point I also started to rebel against the notion that God can't be comprehended, that he can't be accessed with our mental abilities. I wanted to get to know God, to know this great entity from where all creation came to exist.

At the beginning, an internal conflict took place. Still I was attached to my former religious teachings in a way, which constantly taught how God communicated religions to humanity in order to help them overcome the ignorance they are living.

Yet what didn't make sense was how God would present various religions that would declare people different, or present some teaching then change into the next.

Looking around, as I came to further understand, it was clear how God, being the source of all that exists, must be present everywhere, in every soul and in every atom. All matter came through him, and hence are all parts of him.

Religion the way it is practiced usually declares people of other sects and religions to be ignorant and sometimes even enemies. How is this even related to the unity which God can only communicate?

God, if is truly the one and only, must and can't exist unless he is the point from where all comes to exist. God is truly the thing that unites absolutely everything, not only the world's nations but whatever exists. It's a lesson of acceptance beyond any other.

Religion can't be a thing that would divide people but a thing that would affirm that we are all one. This is the only sensible way. The only thing that would divide us hence, is the grudges we hold and our needs for power and for proving ourselves right, which simply arise because we are at a struggle with our selves' worth.

Mohammed treated those who hurt him with great love. Jesus kept affirming that one should love his enemy, Moses affirmed that "*People should listen to their enemies for God is talking*", and so did all other great masters. They had no grudge in their hearts, no anger animated in their actions, they knew that God is present everywhere, and so they just played their role in trying to raise the consciousness of those who were around them, not by thinking or planning, but by being the divine being we all are.

The fact that we are all one, and the presence of various religions which seem to be different, indeed causes a conflict to arise. Is there a single true way or can we just declare all ways to be true? God after all is in every person and in every say.

In here a challenge of thought is required. God, the origin, is present everywhere, in this material realm and in all other realms. God is existence.

It is indeed hard to explain God with words, language as we know it is a flow of mind. We have lost the ancient ways to communicate whole-fully. Probably this is why the ancients communicated in symbols and pictures, not in words as we do today. God can only be experienced, he can't be explained with words; because he is the place where all meet, where all is still, an ecstatic state of mere existence.

As human beings live in this lower material realm, we became unaware that humans, and the creatures we see, are not the only living things in this existence. The vastness of this material world alone suggests the existence of limitless intelligent beings and creatures, and the fact that this material realm is just a level of many suggests as well that our knowledge of what exists is like a drop of water in an infinite ocean.

By examining the ancient scriptures, as many scientists are doing today, it's clear how to the ancients it was quite normal to be in contact with other intelligent beings; sometimes they called them gods (as in ancient Sumer, Greece and even Arabia). They acknowledged that these 'gods' had powers that far exceeded that's of man.

Reports from the Torah and the Bible tell stories that are closer to fiction. Stories chained back to Mohammed report the existence of other creatures in man's early time, the stories report battles that took place between armies of giants, angels, demons and other mighty creatures.

The detailing of these encounters isn't the point here, it's clear that whether in this realm or in other realms, there are other forms of more and less developed beings in terms of awareness and power. Man in the early times was aware of that, he in fact communicated with these beings, served and worshiped them at points and fought with them at others.

These sensible realities, when accepted, open the door for one to perceive farther into the reality of our present. It can't make sense that God would present a religion and then change it into another. He would only communicate true knowledge, which should be unchangeable.

In the case of human beings, it seems that when our physical presence came to exist, with the intellectual ability we have, humans were expected to follow the logical thing, the instinct which clearly shows the difference between what should be done and what would only lead to a dead end. Instead of living our instincts however, we kept sinking in ignorance.

Our inability to recognize our nature caused feelings of worthlessness to start arising. We started comparing ourselves to others, thus bringing up the needs for material and social affirmations. Everyone can tell the rest of the story.

Falling into these traps, humans started diverting farther and farther from their instincts, we became worse than animals as animals need not a religion to help them maintain order, they constantly live their role and their instincts.

And here, beings with higher states of awareness found it in their role to help humans recognize the higher truths, hoping that it would help them change direction instead of destructing their life and the life of the planet they live in.

And so the first religion, or 'law', was passed, asserting that the true path is the path of virtue, the path of knowing the self, knowing the source of all that exists. Special people were chosen to communicate the message; those whom we call 'Prophets'. They were chosen as they were already seeking the higher knowledge, trying to depart from their social ignorance into a collective truth, and a sensible understanding.

But unfortunately, people still didn't listen. They didn't get the point, and so kept descending further and further. Until another act of mercy took place, another 'law' was passed, more restrictions were implied, and more miracles were shown in an attempt to assert the existence of a higher knowledge. Humans however didn't seem to respond much.

And so came another one, and another one, until Islam was presented, a law that covered even the tiniest details, showing how ignorant and untrustworthy humans have become. If one dies for example, his money is shown exactly how to be divided between his wife, children and relatives. We aren't even trusted to make a sane judgment in regard of such simple task. This is where we are now.

Religion isn't the point; it's an act of mercy that has flown to us through higher beings, and to them through the single source that is present in all of us. Even with a religion that presented laws for even the tiniest details, we still failed to restore harmony. Now, Islam is divided into countless sects, each claiming to be on the right path. And Muslim teachers, instead of affirming the essence, are arguing over the silliest details.

The presentation of religions to guide humanity is much like the laws a teacher would imply on a misbehaving classroom, if they are sane enough to see what's good for them, they are left to freely expand their creative expression. When they show signs of ignorance, a teacher might try to help manage their behavior by implying certain laws.

Ali bin Abu Taleb, the cousin and a true disciple of Mohammed's, always affirmed that religion is not the point, that with the mind alone man can see the difference between right and wrong, that religion is just an act of great mercy to help us back into what we have lost.

It's time to see the point. It's time to see why Mohammed kept stating that an hour of meditation is worth more than 70 years of constant religious practice. Knowing the self, and knowing this existence is the key out of our ever destructive behavior. It's how we can take our place back, and grow out of this crude material existence into a finer heavenly-like reality.

By causing religion to be another station for conflict, we are doing the exact opposite of what it came to acknowledge. No amount of prayers or fasting can take anyone to heavens, only what's in our hearts would allow us to experience such finer states.

The only path is the path that would support this revolution in awareness, this is religion, this is God, and God can't but be this. The path is a path into a true universal unity. We are as God is, one.

The Place to Start

It's apparent as the sun is to me that if one's emotional conflicts are resolved, one would become as children are, springs of the moment and fountains of endless energy.

Children are a live expression of what a healthy emotional state can bring out. Their happiness is not bound by a material or social status. They can utilize and enjoy almost anything, their energy is a flow of creativity and a potential of no limits. However, this boundless energy is soon to start fading as parents start pushing the conflicts they have into their children's heads.

One can only teach what he knows, and though a parent might think he is educating his child, unless he himself is rid of his own problems, he will only be leading his child to become a copy of what he already is.

It's clearly observed how children gradually start losing their vitality as they become members of their mainstream. The same cycle is always repeated, only heading for worse consequences as more troubled people are pushed into the society, and more ignorance degrades the collective consciousness of the world.

Since our early childhood, we have learned to repress our feelings. Kids are told not to cry, not to play, to stop making noise, to do this and to stop doing that. Some grow to believe that they do not measure to a sibling or a parent, females sense great discrimination between them and their male peers, some grow to think that they are ugly, losers, fat, dark skinned etc. It's a vicious reality we're all experiencing.

More and more conflicts are imposed through the peers – who have undergone the same parental dilemmas. More is imposed by the schools, by the mainstream's media and by the society.

Gradually, we are programmed into believing that a certain social standard must be met in order for us to measure up. And sadly, almost each one of us falls into the traps of this mindset.

The youth of the society experiences the greatest amount of confusion, being lost between parental and social expectations, each showering them with stereotypes of those whom are most popular and accepted.

There are no definitions for a good stereotype and a bad one, they still are standards that one should measure up to or away from in order to feel good about himself, in order to be a social fit. Whether the standard involved a religious practice, an educational degree, a sport, a music skill or a fashionable style, they all behave the same way for the individual.

Adults also abide by the same social stereotypes. Men require power, money or even religious status in order to measure up. And women, whom are particularly abused, are expected – almost forcibly – to follow what the society wants of them, at times asked to look, shape their bodies and dress in a certain way, and at times confined into social prisons through the teachings of a culture or the interpretation of a religious scripture.

Looking around, one can clearly see the striking resemblance in look and behavior among the peers of a social circle; people dress the same, behave the same, as if they were copies of the same template. Almost everywhere in the world today, individuality is lost.

It requires a lot of awareness to stop and observe how there are no requirements for one to feel good about himself, to see how only the divine presence, this consciousness we have, is enough to confirm that each and every one of us is just the same, only animating through a different level of awareness. The rest, how one looks, what one knows and possesses become just part of the role we are to play. The rich needs to be aware in order to know where his possessions are to be placed, so should the poor in order to see where his gift of energy should flow. We simply need to realize why we came to be what we are and what lessons we need to learn. We are simply asked to be ourselves, hence realizing and becoming the role we are most fit for.

Even while becoming more and more aware, one might still suffer the persistence of his old habits and mental conditions. A lot of people for example, believe that they have attained a certain state of spiritual grace, only to discover later that the state they were living is also another mind trick covering the feelings they weren't able to deal with.

The moral is very simple; repressed feelings will remain a driver of one's actions until they are realized. One should be transparent and freely express how he feels. There should be no compliments or compromises; we should simply be who we are at all times.

If this natural expression is hindered, the unexpressed energy becomes caged like a wild animal into our psyche thus turning into what we call a 'mental illness'. Kids start showing rebellious behaviors, antisocial perhaps, others become shy and think of themselves to be socially misfit. Adults start experiencing forms of depression, they develop forms of conscious and unconscious hatred, they develop obsessions, might become part of a sect or a movement, turn to alcohol, smoke, drugs etc.

Repressing the feelings won't cease them to exist; it will only transform them from their natural form into another veiled one, usually becoming a building block for more conflicts to come.

When one expresses how he feels, the natural instinct is restored. Incessant, angry and rebellious actions cease to exist, and soon one is back into a natural balance.

For all these unconscious feelings to surface, a lot of digging might be required. Conflicts, feelings, sounds and gestures sometimes dating back to the earliest months of our childhood reside and control our habits and motives. We might not be aware of them at the moment, but gradually they become more and more lucid as we get clearer with how we truly feel.

Some exercises help in surfacing these emotions to our awareness, and with my experience, I can say they are quite a necessity.

One of the best exercises we have come to experiment with involves sitting and starting to chant a sad melody, one can chant freely as long as the melody resonates with one's wounds. Keep chanting and gradually feel how the chanted melody becomes the feeling rather than just a harmonic sound, start expressing these feelings more and more with the sounds you chant. And when you feel like it, slow down into silence, and once so, open your eyes and keep them opened, stare into the void in front of you, and feel how the feelings become more and more surfaced, usually causing the eyes to start crying. You might not be aware what exact memories are causing this to happen. For the time – as it's not important - just allow the feelings to surface and the eyes to express.

Sometimes one might experience severe tension in the eyes; they might start flapping up and down quickly. If it happens, just allow them to relax and cry, they are being shut by the pre-imposed psychological and social inhibitions.

After a while, and while the eyes are still expressing, start chanting the melody again, this time, it will be more apparent how the sound of the chant is shaping to express the feelings. Let go and allow yourself to chant what you feel with the melody. Allow the body to move if it wants to, the hands to express and the sound to rise up and down whenever the feeling is stronger or weaker.

The second time you chant will be stronger than the first one, allow it to continue until you feel like slowing down again, and then gradually voice down into silence and open your eyes. As you sit in silence, you will notice how the feelings surface in a clearer way. The eyes usually start crying heavily. Just let go and surrender into the experience. Remain in this state of silence, keeping the eyes open, until you feel that you have expressed what is needed for the time.

This exercise, as we've experienced, is one of the best ways to allow our feelings to surface. You should be aware that the effect might prevail for few days after the exercise is performed. Do not feel embarrassed if tears start running out when in a social circle, just explain, laugh perhaps and allow the expression to flow out.

There is no time or specific schedule for the application of this exercise. One should just keep applying it until he feels satisfied that most feelings have been surfaced, even if the origin of these feeling isn't yet remembered.

This exercise is paired with another one which is later to be explained in this book, one should however start here, apply it few times, before he continues.

If this exercise is wholeheartedly applied, a great transformation in one's behavior and psychological state is observed in a matter of mere days. You might notice a change in your behavior, your interaction with people and in the way you enjoy your time. It will be felt how the change isn't caused by a mind-enforcement trick but through a deeper change, or better said a return of one's naturalness.

The more we surface and express our hidden feelings, the more we clean our subconscious hindrance, clearing the way for our instinct to flow, and for our actions to be an act of natural harmony.

Only then, we stop becoming a destructive animal, whose actions are only serving his mental traumas. Only then we become ready to use our higher intelligence to help raise the consciousness of the existence we came to interact with. This is how serious it is to release the accumulated emotional hindrance.

Sexual Repression

The conflict with our sexuality is a story that is almost 10,000 years old. It is probably the greatest of the taboos we have come to establish, a taboo that is carved not only into our psyche but evidently into our very physical cells.

Ironically, it is apparent that sex is the source of all life on this planet. It is clearly the way by which creatures continue to exist. Whoever started educating the inhibition of human's sexuality, knew exactly what consequences it would bring unto the human's psyche.

Animals never seem to grow obsessed with sex, their interaction is always natural and fulfilled. Only humans – though supposed to be more intelligent into realizing their nature – seem to have grown a problem with this natural instinct. What we fail to see however, due to our limited observation, are the effects which arise when the course of this primary instinct is hindered or obstructed.

In the early years of the twentieth century, great observations that linked sexual oppression with the development of mental illness took place. The study of human psychology was leaping to a new level, and psychoanalysis was formed by Freud and a group of his inner circle. It was clearly observed how sexual repressions led to the development of various physical and psychological diseases. At a point, Freud declared the existence of a biological energy in the body, an energy that flows and nourishes the body, and if obstructed would be the basis for neurosis, that is a mental illness.

This theory however, was denied later on, and the biological investigation for the interaction between sexuality and mental illness became greatly limited. The sudden and strange change in direction is clearly explained - to me at least - by the following observations of another scientist.

Wilhelm Reich, at the time, was a disciple in Freud's inner circle. His observations let him convinced that there is indeed a biological energy that seemed to be hindered in neurotic patients thus accumulating and becoming mental problems, and even manifesting into physical forms. This set the path for him to start a set of biological experiments that further confirmed the connection between the sexual intercourse and flows of electrical, and later to be seen, other form of unknown biological energy.

In the laboratory, he saw how the bodies of his subjects' charged and discharged electrical currents during the course of sexual excitation. He also observed how this natural flow of energy in the body was hindered in the patients who accumulated a great deal of emotional –primarily sexual - inhibitions, the block the energy's natural flow even manifested into muscular tensions that formed as a mean of unconscious defense mechanism to the intensity of the emotions, later referred to by Reich as an 'Armor'.

The relation between humans repressed emotions and the development of psychological (and into physical) illness was very clear. Reich's work *"The Biological Investigation of Sexuality and Anxiety"* offer complete details for these experiments.

Reich then took a step further, and started observing the same dynamics in animals and in micro-biological animal forms.

He started observing how little primitive forms of life, like amoeba, undergo a course of electrical tension and release that support the process of their growth, when became charged they contracted physically, and when discharged they expanded.

Realizing more the energetic basis, he started helping his patients to recover this natural process and to remove any mental and physical blocks that hindered the energy from flowing naturally in and through the body.

The patients, who were able to surrender completely to the sexual experience, started trembling and burst into expressing an immense deal of anger and violence. Because they were instructed to feel the sexual experience rather than rush to a quick 'blow', their anxieties surfaced and burst.

What came to follow was probably the most interesting part in the process. After the immense bursts, patients experienced a state of graceful relaxation unlike anything previously experienced. They felt higher forms of peace and pleasure, strange currents of heat started streaming through their bodies and they felt like they were aware of all that existed around them. Reich soon recognized and declared this to be the actual sexual 'orgasm', the natural gratification which should be experienced during the normal – uninhibited – sexual intercourse, unlike the pervious recognition of orgasm as a state of climax followed by an ejaculation. It became clear that what most people experience today in their sexual intercourse is just another way to run away from one's feelings, that's why the climax is rushed. Therefore, as it's clearly seen, sexual hunger in today's world prevails, even increases and becomes more deformed, the number of times one is engaged in a sexual intercourse doesn't seem to help feed the hunger of its subject, it appears to make it even worse.

Reich was particularly interested in the strange currents of heat that followed the genuine orgasmic experience. The streaming form of energy was clearly not of an electrical nature. It was a different form of energy, unexplainable by the conceptions of physics at the time. He was fortunate enough to be able to carry out a series of laboratory experiments that confirmed the existence this form of energy. He was able to take actual photographs of it, appearing like a bluish haze of glow.

In his microbiological experiments, he came to even more intriguing discoveries, while examining the disintegration of plant life in water – a piece of grass for example – he observed the disintegrating layers of grass transforming into a small circular 'amoebic like' vesicles. The vesicles then seemed to attract this bluish form of energy around them. They glowed with a bluish aura, and later became a living form of amoeba. It was definite to him, that this emerging life form came to exist only through the presence of water, the disintegrated organic material and the bluish form of energy that existed around it.

After performing numerous experiments, Reich declared this new form of energy to being a universal life force. He called it Orgone, and continued to carry out many experiments that further confirmed the existence and the role of this energy in the presence of physical life.

Reich was sadly opposed by his peer colleagues. He was forced out of the psychoanalytic circle, and received death threats which forced him to leave Germany. He fled to Russia, thinking that the communist society was ready for his ideas as they sought equality for people. Few years later, he received similar threats forcing him to escape to America, again, thinking it to be the land of the free where he would be able to carry out his experiments. Few years later he was jailed and died mysteriously in prison, his writings were banned and almost 80 tons of his books were immediately incinerated.

Such an extreme reaction would be understood case he formed a national threat with a deadly weapon or a political move. Reich however was only a wholehearted scientist who sought to discover the nature of things and to help people relieve their psychological illnesses into becoming happy and balanced.

His discoveries did however hit upon the deepest of truths, and so, he was able to set the shortest of paths for people to shift back their imbalances, thus liberating them from their psychological transferences, without which, social hierarchies and movements become impossible to follow.

This clearly didn't act in the best interest of the German revolution at his time, and so, he was forced out of Germany. In Russia where he went next, the government observed how the practices of Reich made his patients 'happy' and with that happiness their interest in the communist revolution faded, though claiming to seek equality for the people, their real motives were apparently – as most other movements are

– methods to gain power and control over the mass of people.

The same happened in America, though the strategy was being performed in a more veiled way, deceiving people into thinking they are free and liberated, yet sucking them into a routine of control through the practices of Capitalism, a vortex of control and corporate enslavement we are experiencing until the day. This control was again feared to be lost by the truths and the methods that were presented by Reich.

I would like to go into further details to explain how the hierarchal control is lost through the performance of these 'almost too simple' practices which Reich came to observe and develop.

As preceded, during the course where Reich urged his patients to relax physically into the natural gratification of the sexual experience, and to avoid rushing for a quick ejaculation. It was ironically observed that instead of experiencing the desired gratification, people started experiencing very extreme bursts of anger and violence, they would start screaming, trembling, pounding and shacking. To the observer it would appear as if a monster is being released to animate through the subject. Those are repressed feelings, most of which are caused by the sexual repressions which have come to be a norm for a long time now.

This great deal of repressed violence, because isn't brought to one's awareness in his everyday life, is instead expressed through other forms of acts and engagements. For example, the interest in warfare in a certain social or religious revolution and the persistence of an anti-social behavior are some forms by which this energy is unconsciously released.

When Reich helped his patients release this repressed energy, naturally, they lost all interests in the social revolutions that took place in their area. It was impossible to fool them into believing that this or that revolution is the way to liberate the people of their society, they lived the inner revolution, and no more caged violence further fed their slavery to those who were abusing it to remain in a position of power.

This is exactly why it's extremely important for us to be liberated of our inner conflicts and repressed emotions, until we are aware of that, all our actions – even the seemingly noble ones

– will be seeds for further destruction, simply because their roots are in most emotional wounds, like begets like.

For you to experience these forms of inner conflicts, we have come to experiment with a simple yet very effective exercise. This exercise will allow one to experience and witness his feelings as they manifest – strangely – to oppose what they are thought to be.

Choose a relaxing music, one that would preferably help you enter a creative and imaginative mood. Lie down and relax completely. Start imagining yourself engaging in your most desired sexual fantasy, let the mind melt, let all inhibitions fade, and allow yourself to experience whatever you find yourself desiring. Enjoy it and flow with it completely. The underlying emotions might not surface in the first session therefore it's encouraged to do more than once, they however usually do in the second session.

Though you would desire a gratifying sexual fantasy, strange feelings of violence and sadism usually start to arise and dominate the experience. Instead of imagining a gratifying intercourse with the partner, one finds himself expressing strange violence against this partner, even if the partner is a loved one. Just allow it to flow and keep expressing whatever feelings are arising, you might imagine hitting the partner, screaming at him or even ripping him apart. Allow the feelings to flow and observe the great deal of violence which stood right in the shadow of your sexual urge, this is exactly why almost no one in the world today seems capable of satisfying his sexual needs. Neither those with sexual freedom nor those with a conservative background are aware that what is being experienced is not a real sexual intercourse and the climax felt is anything but a true orgasm, they are just quick ways to blow some of the steam out, and until the underlying emotions are realized, no true satisfaction will be attained and more and more mental illness will keep building up.

Some of the world's leaders are very aware of these facts, and through the plantation of wrongful understandings of the sexual nature, they allow for great deals of sadism and masochism to be planted into the minds of the societies, enabling those leaders to control the mass for a movement, a revolution or to just keep them torn apart in egotistical conflicts.

I believe it comes clear now why Reich, along with anyone who walked his steps were greatly opposed and literally wiped out the pages of our common history.

There are no limits for the forms of mental illnesses that would arise through the repression of this primary biological need and the implantation of mental misconceptions about it. Hatred arises and violence becomes rooted in the society, starting at the earliest years of the youth's adolescence. Deformed sexual inclinations, the rage of the youth, anti-social behaviors, sadism, masochism, enjoying bloodshed or violence, depression, mistreatment of women, hunger for material and social growth are but some examples of what can come out.

Unfortunately, great deal of this ignorance is being imposed through the religious leaders, the very people who are meant to embrace our instincts as a product of God and an act of natural harmony. Clearly and sadly, violent urges are usually seen most apparent among the practitioners of a close-minded religion. They may claim to be fighting for a cause, yet failing to see how their anger is not serving the cause but is just a reflection of their own personal frustration.

The same is observed in controlled armies and in tribal societies, where the members, males particularly, are isolated and confined to certain practices and initiations since their early years.

James DeMeo, a follower of Reich's work, spent years of his life excavating and deciphering the ruins of ancient civilizations. He came to observe that at the early times of man, almost 10,000 years back, the societies of the world used to live peacefully and almost no wars took place, it seemed as if humans were living in a golden age, until suddenly, the social and religious teachings started taking a different direction. Sex started to become a taboo and children were initiated into thoughts of guilt and repression against their natural feelings, which is much like what we are doing to our children today. In the same era: artifacts, ancient drawings and documents of humans engaging in wars started to come into view. This is not believed to be a coincidence.

It's interesting to note that other changes also accompanied such changes in perceptions.

Males started to dominate societies, when before, women were considered the mothers of their societies. Children became dominated by families, particularly by the father, when before they lived in a social democracy and were raised by a commune. Women became oppressed instead of being equal to men. Religions started to become 'pain seeking' oriented. Homosexual and incent tendencies started to arise, and so on.

Perhaps this is why Reich stated that 'natural love' was extinguished from the hearts of humans since more than 10,000 years. It's clear that he knew and observed the transformation that took place during the period.

The preceding statement is particularly important to bring to our attention. For the matter, I'll try to explain further with few common examples.

As it is seen, thousands of people are getting married each day. Though the married couple might be madly in love before becoming 'legal' partners, soon after the marriage and after a usual period of two or three months, the love starts fading and the partners start building up massive confusions as they experience their love turning into a strange hatred. It is a sad case, and what makes it even sadder is the fact that most couples remain married for a long time even after their love ceases to exist. They become miserable and might even start seeking love elsewhere.

Similar cases are observed among almost all lovers today. One day a person might be madly in love, and the next he is bursting with anger, blame and hatred. This happens simply because the experience before wasn't a true state of love and graceful acceptance, but an expression and a projection of one's emotional void unto the other. As soon as this partner fails in being the anticipated savior, or challenges with an opposing thought, he becomes a target on whom all frustrations would pour.

This is why people seem to be addicted to dramatic emotional situations; they might express it in a relationship, in a form of music, by watching movies or shows, by reading stories, poetry etc. It's all a product of the same thing. If one lived in grace, these emotional expressions will simply stop making sense and a more natural 'child like' state will come in place.

Therefore and again, getting to know ourselves and becoming aware of our feelings is the first step one should take in order for a real change to come. The method by which this is accomplished is irrelevant, being honest with ourselves and with others – by being a live expression of our thoughts and feelings – is the goal and is the way by which balance is restored. Afterwards, it becomes much easier for the one who's interested in advancing his state of awareness to continue the path.

Reich wrote once in a letter to a friend of his:

"I'm fully capable of working, hating, and loving, and I fear only being tied to a neurotic situation that could drag me along with it. On the whole, I'm very calm and the only thing I am fighting against is the need to armor myself. I'm afraid that in the process I will lose my best intuitive qualities. That's serious!"

Feelings are a form of energy, and unless expressed they would be transformed elsewhere causing an imbalance and forming neurotic symptoms. It was clear to Reich that for one to be natural, for the intuitive qualities to be present and for the neurotic symptoms and muscular armoring to dissolve, one should train himself to be expressive at all times.

It is believed that more than 90% of our neurotic symptoms are caused by the great deal of sexual repression and the misconceptions we have picked over the years of our lives and especially during our early years. Sex is managed directly by the flow of our life force and the underlying misconceptions cause a primary disturbance in the flow of this energy, the very same energy that is managing life in our physical presence. This is why the issue is particularly stressed out, and this is why this is the main contributor to whatever mental imbalance we have come to develop.

To help get familiar with the internal manifestations of these struggles and to help release them, the following exercise is very important:

Choose a private place, lie down and start breathing, let the breath grow deeper and deeper making sure you are feeling relaxed and comfortable with the breath's rhythm. It's important for the breath to be deep enough to comfortably fill your entire lungs, keep breathing and during the time start feeling your tension surfacing, you might find yourself starting to vocalize the tension and the pain as you breath out, a sound similar to "*Aah*" is most common. Keep breathing and feel how the pain becomes more surfaced, and the sound becomes more and more intense. Try to feel your entire body and become aware of any existing muscular tensions, the tension is usually most apparent in the neck, shoulders, eyes, and the jaw. You can put your fingers on the tensed muscle and press against it; this will help release the tension but might cause sudden emotional bursts, which is particularly good for the process.

At this point there will be challenges to stop and retreat, just keep breathing at all costs and slowly you will feel your whole body reacting with the process, when you feel yourself reaching to a peak, open your eyes and allow yourself to explode. The explosion in this exercise is stronger than any other you might have witnessed. One usually and uncontrollably starts screaming, your whole body might start trembling, allow it to shake, to move in any direction it wants, hit the ground or move up and down. Just explode!

While you are exploding, you might become aware of the exact memories that are causing this pain to present. It is here where people usually experience visual pictures from the earliest times of their childhood, where the actual sources of one's mental problems become apparent.

Let yourself flow completely with the experience. Eventually it starts slowing down and one enters a deep state of rest. A great feeling of awareness would usually accompany that state and you might feel streams of gentle heat moving through your body. Just relax into the experience, even allow yourself to sleep and rest.

The impact of releasing one's tension will be clearly and immediately experienced. One's need to judge other individuals will diminish, as would the need to feel better than others, either by advancing materially, psychologically or by demeaning other people. It will be easier to love everyone unconditionally, there will be no more needs to argue and it will be easier to live and be aware of the present moment as the hidden burdens are no more present. This is the first step into becoming a human. Here is the release of our most dominant emotional burdens. It is a priceless gift if one is aware enough to admit to himself and see.

Islam

Growing up, we have learned to appreciate the great days of glory Muslims have lived in their early years. We were told stories of how Arabs led the advancement of science in the world for hundreds of years, how they were great philosophers and how their civilization presented the peak in cultural and material development in that era.

Those days were constantly glorified and compared with the present ignorance Muslims and Arabs are living, and it was anticipated that those days would be relived again someday soon.

One day however, and while we were being educated about a small period in the Islamic history which followed the death of the prophet Mohammed, three lines in our course book mentioned a small battle that took place between two parties, a party that was lead by one of Mohammed's grand children, Al Hussein, and another Muslim party. The paragraph barely mentioned the name of the battle 'Karbala', the date and where it took place.

Though the lesson continued without any slight emphasis on the incident, I couldn't but pause and wonder if I heard what I heard correctly!

The first shock – to me – was the fact that two Muslim parties fought each other at such an early time, and the second was that some people 'who were considered Muslims' stood in the way of the prophet's grandson, whose great virtues needed not an introduction.

I asked the teacher about it, who shut me up by saying that these issues should not be raised as they are mere 'Shia' issues. For those who are not familiar, Sunnah and Shia are the two major Islamic sects, in our area; the Sunnah sect was the prevalent one, and the Shia – naturally – was vilified.

My interest lied not in a sect or a conflict however, I just couldn't understand how such thing could take place, especially that we were taught to look up to those past days of glory, and to almost every person who lived in and around that era, the era of the direct disciples of the prophet.

I started to dig into all the resources I could find, the findings weren't simple and shook my entire ground. For a starter, I learned that the battle mentioned earlier wasn't in fact a battle, Al Hussein was traveling with his expanded family – wives and children included – when they were met in the middle of the way by an army of opposing 'Muslims' who surrounded them, drove them to extreme hunger and thirst, and then killed all their men and most of their male children, including the prophet's grandson, who was beheaded and whose body was brutally stepped over with the enemies' horses.

The incident was traumatic enough to paralyze my thoughts for a while, and after, I continued to search into the roots of this great irony, of this great disrespect to the prophet's very direct family and by the very people whom were later to be considered leaders of the Islamic advancement. Those simply didn't sound like days of glory, and no attempt of my peers or teachers seemed to provide a convincing answer, I couldn't even believe they were trying to justify the incident!

Digging into the roots, I learned that a great conflict took place as soon as the prophet died. The following Muslim head, Abu Bakr, was chosen away and while the prophet was being buried. His cousin, Ali bin Abu Taleb (Al

Hussein's father) was one of people whom were burying the prophet, and was completely struck to know that most of the Muslims, even at the very time of the burial, were busy fighting over a new leader.

Ali bin Abu Taleb, retreated to his home and didn't accept what happened, spending almost six months before he acknowledged Abu Bakr as a leader for the Islamic community.

The Shia Muslims believe that Ali bin Abu Taleb should have been the first leader to follow Mohammed. They provide various situations where Mohammed – indirectly – declared Ali to be the wisest among Muslims, and the doorway to the divine knowledge that is being channeled through him.

There is much dispute about this, and here lies not the point. The point is to observe the great conflicts that took place then, which clearly reflect the level of people's awareness even at that early time. Ali bin Abu Taleb kept stating that what started with such great conflict, with such hunger for power, will only lead to a great destruction, opposing the very thing Islam was supposed to be about. And so it did.

Abu Bakr was followed by Omar bin Al Khattab, and Omar was followed by Othman bin Affan. All of whom are believed to have led wholeheartedly. During Othman's time however, great conflicts started to take place between the Muslims due to Othman appointing members of his family, who proved to be deceitful men of politics rather than of virtue and awareness. The conflicts rose more and more violent and were ended by the murder of Othman at his very home.

After Othman's tragic death, Muslims asked for Ali to become the next leader, who kept refusing and saying *"What do you want me to do now after you have sunk into such level?!"*. Eventually he accepted however, though knowing the great conflicts that are yet to come.

Trying to pull the shattered pieces of the Islamic community, Ali was opposed by Moawiyah bin Abu Sufian, a relative of Othman whom he appointed the chief of Sham (area where Syria is now). Moawiyah was a very intelligent man, a man of politics however. He knew that Ali was aware of that, and to keep his position, he had to play some tricks, otherwise, he knew very well that he would be one of the first people to be replaced.

Moawiyah refused to accept Ali's position as the new leader for the Islamic community; he said that Ali was responsible for the death of his cousin Othman, although Ali and his sons were some of the few people who stood at the very door of Othman's house, defending his life.

And so, Moawiyah refused to unite with other Muslims into declaring Ali bin Abu Taleb the new Muslim leader, and even encouraged the inhabitants of his area to declare him a leader instead, showering them with material and social temptations.

Ali bin Abu Taleb, who desperately tried to unite all Muslim parties failed to get through to Moawiyah. The records of their letters are still kept to the day in the books of history, and to the willing reader, it's clear how Ali was desperately urging Moawiyah to see the higher truth, while Moawiyah was only trying to play games of politics in order to ensure staying in his position.

What came to follow can be easily imagined, the details – even the accuracy of the events - are not important, the point is simple, and with it holds a great wisdom not only for Muslims but for every other religion, cult and hierarchy of power.

Ali bin Abu Taleb, who had a true divine understanding, knew exactly what would happen when he saw the ignorance of the Islamic community animating, he tried to communicate that to the people, but their awareness was sadly not ready to see beyond their hunger for tribal and material power.

What happened had nothing to do with the truths which Islam came to reassure. It was the same story which has been, and is still being repeated since thousands of years. The story of the human who fails in knowing himself, in knowing the sources of his conflicts and needs, and so is trying to assure his value with the pursuance of material and social powers.

Ali bin Abu Taleb was a true master, his words speak for his wisdom, through which he clearly assured how Islam is just another way that is supposed to lead back into the human's natural instinct. The Islamic teachings today, sadly, have almost nothing to do with what Islam – or any religion – is about. Muslims are lost in empty practices and in disputes about the interpretations of the Quran's verses and the records of Mohammed. If Muslims were to understand the essence, there won't be a Sunnah sect or a Shia sect. Muslims will all be united under the same divine truth. Furthermore, there won't be a Muslim, a Christian, a Jew, or a Buddhist as the universal instinct will be enough to make it clear that the truths these religions came to assure are all one, all disputes and needs for arguments come from our wounded selves.

Mohammed assured over and over that Islam is about virtue, that Islam is the religion of the instinct. There were many incidents where he stated that an hour of true meditation is worth more than 70 years of constant religious practice. He told Muslims that they will divide into as many as 73 sects, all of whom are ignorant except one, who will walk the way of the prophet Abraham, a prophet whose entire life was spent in contemplation for a better understanding of this universe, and the source of its existence.

There can be no other true religion than a one which would assure the unity of all people, and of all creatures. God is one, he is the source, and all that exists is a spring that has come through this single point.

This is what religions came to say, it's time to see that.

What is Happiness

If one would think of the best think to ask for, happiness would be the only worthy thing to come to mind.

What's the worth of all material possessions, of fame and of power if one led a miserable life? We are witnessing countless examples of people who attained the highest levels of material power and social popularity, only to end up committing suicide or sinking into depression, alcoholism and drugs.

I don't believe anyone would choose this over a simple happy life, there is simply no point in all the possessions if they failed to bring a state of happiness. Our pursuance for more material possessions and more social status in the first place, is nothing but a desperate attempt to become happier. If they too failed to do that, even sunk us to a more miserable state, then what's the point?

Happiness isn't dependent on a material condition; it's a state of present gracefulness, an utter joy of being.

It is particularly important to observe how people mistake true joy for the fake state of happiness where peaks of excitement are felt. That's not happiness, it's just the opposite of sadness, the other peak of the pendulum, and it's always observed that right after such peak, one sinks to the other pole, into the sad state. The Quran mentions in one of its verses that "*God doesn't like those who live states of extreme happiness*".

True happiness is right in the middle between the two. It is neither a state of excited happiness nor a state of sadness. Joy is a better word to describe that state, a state of peace where one is simply graceful, a state of living in the present, of thoughtlessness, and of letting go.

Osho, a great enlightened master once said:

"*The desire for happiness simply shows that you are not happy right at this moment. The desire for happiness simply shows that you are a miserable being, and a miserable being projects in the future that sometime, someday, someway, he will be happy. Out of misery comes your projection. It carries the very seeds of misery. It comes out of you, it cannot be different from you. It is your child, its face will be like you. In its body your blood will be circulating. It will be your continuity.*

You are unhappy today; you project tomorrow to be happy, but tomorrow is a projection of you, of your today, of whatsoever you are. You are unhappy, the tomorrow will come out of this unhappiness and you will be more unhappy. Of course, out of more unhappiness you will desire for more happiness in the future again. And then you are in a vicious circle: the more unhappy you become, the more you desire for happiness; the more you desire for happiness, the more unhappy you become. Now it is like a dog chasing its own tail.

So the first thing is not to dream, not to project. The first thing is to be herenow. Whatsoever it is, just be herenow – and a tremendous revelation is waiting for you. The revelation is that nobody can be unhappy in the herenow."

This sums it all.

True Masters

True masters have been misunderstood, tortured, killed, cursed and declared crazy throughout history. This happened to almost every spiritual master we have come to know, let not mention those whom we missed. Ironically, briefly after their death, they become recognized, sadly however as an 'icon' and not by following the true wisdom they came to acknowledge and the path they undertook in their journeys.

This is only a natural consequence, simply because those masters challenged the ignorance their people lived in. Not by opposing, but by simply showing the higher truths people were missing. Because this challenged the hierarchy of power, and the pride of people, they resorted to the quick opposition for these masters. And so people kept growing more ignorant of the self, more destructive and more miserable.

Pride is nothing but a desperate attempt to assign value to one's self, the place where this comes from is clear and is examined earlier in this book. A person who has grown to know himself, to know the nature of his being, needs not a sense of pride, for he knows his true value, his divine nature, and so is able to see its presence in him and in every other person and creature.

Naturally, the people whom are being glorified today are those who are in the highest material and social positions. Yet those who have found the truth and are living the peace we are all desperate to have are strangely scolded and abandoned. It's a product of our ignorance and blindness to the real worth of things.

No one would choose a piece of dirt over a priceless gem. Let's just stop for a moment and review what we truly want, what's worthy and what isn't.

The first step, again, is to look into ourselves, to recognize our deep fears and wounds, and to express and dissolve them. Only then we can remove that which is blinding us, and only then we can see what can truly bring us joy.

There should be no fears or oppositions to the governments and parties who are trying to help maintain this state of ignorance and to further brainwash the mainstream through the medias, commercialism, social temptations etc. It's us who are allowing this to happen. For example, having an emotional wound, one might be tempted to buy something for a triple of its worth. The increase in cost might allow him to assign a little more value to his unfelt self worth, a wound is acting. Such act would sound extremely silly to the aware one, who would only place a bid for the real worth of the object, having no underlying – unexpressed – emotions to overshadow his natural instincts. He would similarly not obtain an object unless a real need for it is present.

These are just more examples to illustrate where our ignorance to what's in us would lead, and what it would cause us to miss.

Enlightenment

A lot of spiritual practitioners aspire to that which the masters of the past have called 'enlightenment', a state where one attains the highest degrees of spiritual and personal mastery.

Enlightenment however is something we already have, yet are only failing to see. The soul, the consciousness we have through which our physical body is brought to life, is the spark of divine mystery and the life that is animating all this existence. It is the instinct, the awareness, the thing that exists beyond time and space, the oneness with the source, and the spring of the single point, of God.

We are already enlightened, only ignorant enough not to see our divine nature. The path to enlightenment has been explained by the ancient wisdom as a road which takes us in a long pilgrimage, only ending where we already are. We are already enlightened; we just fail to be aware of that.

This is essential to realize, as many spiritual practitioners fall into pursuing a spiritual experience or an expression of a form of paranormal power. All such are just presentations of mere science, though uncommonly known to our age. Truth is beyond science and is beyond the mind, it lies in the nothingness and thoughtlessness of the present. The shift is a shift of awareness.

Our thoughts are the creators of our reality. We think that many actions, journeys and learning need to take place before we can evolve. But fail to see that the only thing needing to be done involves a present change in our perceptions and thoughts. We don't need to go anywhere, or learn anything in order to advance; we only need to change our present perceptions, because they are the only inhibitors of whatever naturalness we should be living. If you want to become happy, then let happiness become your present. Feel it and become it. You will see how no action needs to be done; only a change of thought is sufficient.

If a lot of hindering emotions are present, they would stand in the way of that change in perception, you might find yourself unable to even imagine yourself being happy, this is why it's always wise to be as clean as a little child; that is by being a live expression of whatever feelings we have.

Enlightenment involves being aware of the totality of this world and of this existence, with it all judgments fall, and everything becomes a teacher. In there, by seeing the oneness in everything and by surrendering to the present, each step becomes a divine step. No planning or mind work would be further needed, as one would be his role and would live the joy of Godliness.

We only need to be aware.

If we don't Wake up

The world is moving at a faster pace now, time is tightening up, and soon we might start experiencing the consequences of our ignorance in the most extreme forms, not only on a human level – as in social conflicts and wars – but on an expanded collective level.

When a person keeps abusing his body with an imbalanced diet and with stressing emotions, it loses its natural harmony and starts developing a cancerous – self destructing – behavior, a last attempt from it to clean its own system.

Earth is starting to do just the same, it's trying to unburden itself, wipe off excess population, fight back the pollution and the limitless abuses we are inflicting on its resources. We are aware of the increasing natural disasters, and these acts of nature will keep worsening unless we start changing our collective consciousness.

Because we have become a very repressed nation, we have developed unconscious sadistic and masochistic feelings. This is also reflecting here, as people seem to be nonchalant even to their own destruction. This is why we don't seem to empathize with what's happening, even knowing that a definite end is near.

This earth will just keep doing what it needs to do, if we don't wake up to the destruction we're inflicting on ourselves and on nature around us, then Earth will try to do the action by wiping us up, it's a simple natural consequence.

Why limit our development? And why spare a graceful living for a miserable one? Death is not the end, our consciousness is ever alive, and we will keep experiencing the consequences of our ignorance until we face the presented challenge and learn the lesson, the lesson that needs to be learned in order for us to take a step further.

In the simple words of this little book lies the resolution to our inner conflicts, a resolution that has been cried out loud by some of the greatest men to have lived. The only thing we need to do is get rid of our unnaturalness, that which took place when we started repressing and inhibiting our free expression. When no more conflicts are resident in us, we will find ourselves naturally stepping back into the natural state of harmony, and then we can start using our intelligence to reverse the damage and further refine this existence.

A further advice is to be told, in the beginning stages, as one starts to realize his underlying conflicts, severe expressions might be experienced. And so, until you are sure that the greatest part of your underlying emotions has been expressed, try to perform these exercises away from people, as you won't want to shout an emotion of anger where it doesn't belong. Let's stop misplacing our emotions and reactions.

When the greatest part of one's emotional reservoir is released, one can act out his present feelings knowing that they are only divine reactions to the present moment. Only then, the instinct is no more shadowed and our ability to judge for the better is restored.

We are only needed to be who we are.

"When I succeeded in concentrating on this single problem for three decades, mastering it and orienting myself within its fundamental natural function, in spite of all obstacles and personal attacks, I began to realize that I had transcended the conceptual framework of the existing human character structure and, with it, our civilization during the past five thousand years. Without wanting to, I found myself outside its limits. Hence I had to expect that I would not be understood even if I produced the simplest and most easily verifiable facts and interconnections. I found myself in a new, different realm of thought, which I first had to investigate before I could go on."

Wilhelm Reich